MW01122422

160201

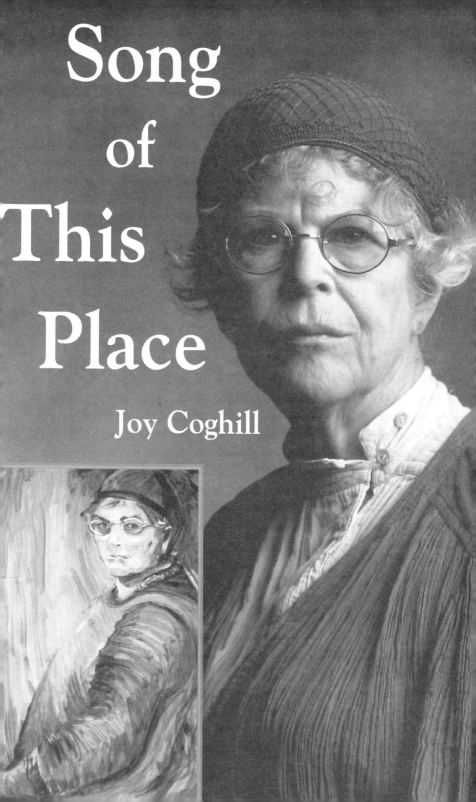

Song

of

This

Place

Joy Coghill

Song of This Place

Joy Coghill

with an introduction by Cynthia Zimmerman

Playwrights Canada Press
Toronto • Canada

Playwrights Canada Press
54 Wolseley St., 2nd fl. Toronto, Ontario CANADA M5T 1A5
416-703-0013   fax 416-703-0059
orders@playwrightscanada.com • www.playwrightscanada.com

Playwrights Canada Press acknowledges the support of
the taxpayers of Canada and the province of Ontario through
The Canada Council for the Arts and the Ontario Arts Council.

Cover painting – Emily Carr "Self-portrait" 1938-1939. National Gallery of
Canada, Ottawa. Gift of Peter Bronfman, 1990.
Cover photo of Joy Coghill by David Cooper Photography.
Production editor/Cover design: Jodi Armstrong

National Library of Canada Cataloguing in Publication

Coghill, Joy
    Song of this place / Joy Coghill.

A play.
ISBN 0-88754-682-X

    1. Carr, Emily, 1871-1945—Drama. I. Title.

PS8555.O293S65 2003   C812'.6   C2003-903341-4
PR9199.4.C64S65 2003

First edition: July 2003.
Printed and bound by AGMV Marquis at Quebec, Canada.

Unfortunately, the mythic side of man is given short shrift nowadays. He can no longer create fables. As a result a great deal escapes him....

Carl Jung

— • — to all the women who dare — • —

— • — *Table of Contents* — • —

— • — *The Artist's Crucible* — • —

Joy Coghill's Song of This Place

by Cynthia Zimmerman

> How is it that
> one star, alone,
> dares.[1]

Not only was Emily Carr the first and the best-known of our women artists, she was one who found fame in her own time. Even more significant, she had a fiercely independent spirit, a vibrant and eccentric nature, and a strong personal vision which her art proclaimed. In *Song of This Place*, the central character actor/playwright Frieda, admires Carr intensely. *Song of This Place* is Frieda's play. While it calls upon the life of Emily Carr, it is essentially a play about Frieda's wish to be worthy and her wish to be able to play the part of Emily Carr.

The idea is that Frieda has written a play in which she will star as Emily Carr. The actor is at a difficult moment in her life and in her career. In a wheelchair and often feeling "too old for this" (17), Frieda is nonetheless pushing forward to this new challenge. She wants, as Carr did before her, to create "the soul stuff" (19), to become a remarkable artist, but she is meeting what seem insurmountable barriers. At this moment she reaches toward Carr, knowing that talent is not enough, that, as Urjo Kareda once said: "[f]inally character is as important as talent."[2]

Given Frieda's age, profession and ambition, it is easy to make the assumption of a powerful autobiographical link, especially since actor/playwright Joy Coghill wrote the part of Frieda for herself. As novelist Graham Swift said recently in a *Globe & Mail* interview, "Personal life is where you begin as a writer" (8 May 03). All artists use "material" from their own lives, from their own struggles and experiences, so it is always a temptation to read into fiction the biographical impulse, whether conscious or unconscious. Naturally one remembers that even in deliberately autobiographical writing there is reworking, inventing, amending, omitting – all the permutations that can come between the fact and the fiction, the art and the life, the plot and the personal story. Nonetheless it is safe to presume a special empathic connection between the creator and the created when one artist depicts the creative process and the professional travails of another. Of course Coghill is not Frieda, or not exactly Frieda. But "policing" documentary evidence may not be the most important thing, as Leigh Gilmore reminds us.[3] In *Song of This Place*, the tension of the space between the actor/playwright Frieda and the actor/playwright Joy Coghill is never far from the surface.

The "Carr passion" led Coghill first to try to find someone to write the play she could star in. When she could not, she undertook to write it herself. This was her first venture into playwriting territory. Her description of her struggle and the breakthrough is illuminating. At the Playwright's Colony in Banff in 1984, Coghill had a late night "visitation" from the indomitable Emily Carr herself:

> So there I was, struggling away in long-hand, getting more and more desperate. I started talking to myself and to Emily too, and I said to her, "Look, its a matter of pride. You've got to help me. You need this play as much as I do. It's just as bad for artists now as it was then, you know. People don't care."
>
> ...So I started having conversations with her, in my head, and writing them down, and that became the basis for the play. And because no-one at Banff could read my writing, it became a one-woman show. [4]

You have got to help me, Coghill says, you need this play as much as I do. In creating Frieda, Coghill addresses the artist's need for recognition as a professional. Coghill's Emily may know about the importance of validation but that does not mean she easily gives it. The fact that Carr never had much respect for actors, for what she called "second-hand living" (23), is one of the challenges the character Frieda will have to confront. Also significant in this passage is the idea of conversation, dialogue and not merger. In various situations and repeatedly the play text refers to "the space between" and the electricity of connection. So what she first imagined as a one-person show would not be, in part because Coghill believes so profoundly that "the art of acting [is] not what any one actor [does] but what happen[s] between them" (xii).

In this late-night encounter, the formidable Emily Carr who came to debate and dialogue with Joy Coghill was, of course, an Emily of her own making – a version of the famous BC artist that could connect to the fears and concerns of this particular struggling writer. Coghill idealized Carr not only because of her immense talent but also because

Carr had "struggled and fought and won" (25). Her Frieda wants the Emily Carr of the "Self-Portrait, 1938," that image of Carr that so many prize: Carr, with "mountain-monumentality,"5 so solid and strong, a natural part of the elemental earth her paintings celebrate.

Song of This Place is about Frieda's journey to artistic freedom and confidence. This is an ordeal undertaken with Carr as adversary, guide and mentor. Frieda, in a wheelchair, is described as *"a passionate, intelligent, self-centred woman, an actress first, a person second"*(7). She is fifty-nine years old, an age significant to Frieda because Emily Carr produced her most significant work after her National Gallery show when she was fifty-six.6 Stage directions state that this play is *"Frieda's vehicle for her old age. It is her way of facing the limitations that begin to menace her"* (8). Coghill's idea of a "one-woman show" undergoes a sea-change: Frieda creates a puppet play. The puppets are to enhance the theatrical magic but, while the actors manipulate them, Frieda will supply all the voices. By so doing she intends to control the stage. The problem is that her idea for the play is not working.

Song of This Place opens in a deep forest where, according to the stage directions, "the spirit of Emily Carr can be found" (3). Frieda has brought her young company here for a rehearsal in the hope of finding "the missing link" (4). She hopes that by entering this space she can get in touch with Carr's spirit, the spirit which she has not been able to generate in her play. During rehearsal Frieda breaks down: she cannot supply the voice for the Emily Carr puppet. It is at this point that the ghost of Emily Carr enters and replaces the puppet. Frieda pleads for Carr's "blessing" (16); without it she cannot access Carr's "voice," her "essence" (20). But Millie, as Carr is called in the play, is not ready to give of herself, to let Frieda "become [her]"(20). First Frieda must know more about Millie's spirit and Millie's way of seeing her art and her life. Before Millie will be open with Frieda she puts Frieda through a series of tests: of her skills as an actor, of her knowledge and perceptiveness, and of her courage. Only after the successful completion of this trial will Millie be willing to share "the soul stuff" (19), the "soul things that cannot be expressed" (23). In Act Two Millie leads Frieda deeper into the forest, deeper into the dangers that accompany such a journey, deeper into the artist's psychic realities, and deeper into herself. It is there that Frieda learns the link between Millie's internal life and her creative process: the inner spiritual work that her art expresses. Ultimately, for every artist, it is "the soul stuff" which births works of enduring value. So it is in the deep interior of the forest that Frieda must find the conviction and the strength to "Sing [her] own song" (34). Then the "transfer" can occur, then it will be possible for "*MILLIE [to give] and FRIEDA [to take] over MILLIE'S 'life' and memory*" (56).

Through Frieda's experience Coghill dramatizes the perilous but essential journey for the artist. It is in the wild woods, or the place of the unconscious, that the artist sees feelingly what is required: the hard work, the act of will, the courage to withstand ostracism and isolation, and the usefulness, if not the necessity, of turning her outsider status into a badge of pride. Emily tells of the time her "light had gone"(18), of how her faith came to be renewed. From 1913 to the mid-twenties, Carr had despaired of her art and hardly painted. She ran a boarding house in Victoria. But the 1927 showing of a number of works at the National Gallery of Canada where she met the Group of Seven, particularly Lawren Harris, revived her. In those moments of despair, Millie says, "You need to receive the right message from a soul that understands..." and Frieda acknowledges, "That is why I'm here" (32). Frieda finally wins the kind of profound validation and inspiration from Emily Carr that Emily received from Lawren Harris.

Ultimately Emily shares with Frieda the most precious thing of all: her unique vision – her way of seeing the forest green and all of life in a unified liveness, a wholeness of unceasing kinetic energy – "That [is] the God in it" (42). This is the theosophy of Lawren Harris and other artists of Carr's time, but it is congenial to our contemporary Frieda, who welcomes the spiritual infusion, the nature-based spirituality. Frieda learns what is meant by the rhythm inherent in each created thing, "the song" of each thing and of "this place." The puppet of her child-self recalls a similar spiritual awakening with her father, years before: "There was a singing happening between those stars and the earth beneath us. That is the only song that matters," her father said. "You must say yes to that song Frieda, the rest is sleep" (55). Frieda takes to heart Carr's message about the artist's role. Now connected to the forest space and to each other, the two elderly artists rejoice together. But the fantastical nature of the play suggests this is a fable. Does it also suggest that the spirituality and the final confirmation by an idealized other, which lies at the heart of the matter, is myth as well?

Frieda has been told, finally, that the confirmation she needs she must supply herself. The confirmation by Emily Carr is a figment of her imagination, a ghost, but so are the demons that undermine her. Just as Coghill had to write the play herself, her protagonist has to find her own voice and sing her own song boldly, despite the naysayers. She must take the risk. "Making art becomes an activity akin to exercising

[her] spirituality, as when Carr wrote of trying in her painting 'to get that joyous worshipping into the woods and mountains'".7 It is her work and her faith which will set Freida free. This is transparently visualized when we see Freida rise from her wheelchair, able now to move, to act and to dance.

In writing *Song of This Place*, Coghill's ambition was to dramatize the path to creative freedom and offer a glimpse into the mysterious workings of the creative imagination. Basing it on the life of Emily Carr, she also wanted to deliver Emily's world in a magical, inventive and unique way. "Theatre needs exciting, new forms in order to fight 'the box!'," she said. Because Coghill wanted to do in the theatre what Emily did in her paintings, that is capture the inner spirit, and because the central action of the play is internal and hence difficult to develop dramatically, she called upon the sister arts—music, puppetry, mime, dance and song—to share in the enterprise. "[I]t has to be [Carr's] standards in my world," Coghill said in a publicity release for the play. Therefore, the original production engaged established artists including director and animator Robert More, composer Bill Henderson for scored as well as improvised music, visual painter Sherry Grauer and Robert Welch for design and lighting, and Frank Rader, master mask and puppet maker, for the twenty masks and puppets required. The script calls for these puppets, who represent the inhabitants of Millie's world, to "grow" with the play: they begin small and voiced by Frieda but, when they come to life, they are voiced first by their manipulators and later, in Act Two, they change into the full-size actors wearing half-masks. Similarly, as the forest gets darker and Frieda's experience more emotionally intense, the lighting and music must rise to meet it – ultimately creating a *mise en scène* that is moving, fluid, richly resonant of the dream rendered vibrantly alive. "We felt," says Coghill, "we were creating a new form of theatre that made extraordinary demands and was deeply satisfying" (xii).

It took five years to bring *Song of This Place* to its opening in September of 1987. It seems most fitting that it opened in a former church, the Vancouver East Cultural Centre. The play, which is mystical at its core, closes with a song which celebrates the liberation possible through creativity. As the artists dance to "The Song of This Place," the play reaches its ultimate realization: the phrase which Emily Carr used to describe her wish to capture the inner life of each created thing, applies equally to Frieda's struggle to incorporate the song of Emily Carr. Thematically and theatrically *Song of This Place* sings of the release, the soaring of the human spirit through art, through creative collaboration, through theatre.

For Coghill, Frieda's story is her story is Emily's story... the particulars change but the essentials of the artist's journey remain. Athol Fugard said the same about his creation of Helen Martins for *Road to Mecca*: "telling her story was telling my story too." Coghill's play is a hybrid: biography, autobiography and fiction. According to Sherrill Grace, Coghill is "pushing the concept of auto\biographical theatre to its core as self-performance."[8] It represents an "artist's crucible" because *Song of This Place* dramatizes moving through the barriers, stripping away the superficial, to come at last to the essential—the core—the pure vision. To what remains after such a process the artist must be true: this is the process by which the alchemist in every artist comes upon his gold.

— • — *Notes* — • —

[1] *Song of This Place*, 25.

[2] Cynthia Zimmerman, "Maintaining the Alternative: An Interview With Urjo Kareda" in *Performing National Identities: International Perspectives on Contemporary Canadian Theatre*. Grace and Glaap, eds. (Vancouver: TalonBooks, 2003), 222.

[3] Leigh Gilmore, *Autobiographics: A Feminist Theory of Women's Self-Representation* (Cornell UP, 1994), 14.

[4] *Playboard*, August 1987.

[5] Sharyn Rohifsen Udall, *Carr, O'Keeffe, Kahlo: Places of Their Own* (New Haven: Yale UP, 2000), 100.

[6] This was the "Canadian West Coast Art" exhibit in Ottawa, 1927, where Emily Carr met Lawren Harris and members of the Group of Seven.

[7] Sharyn Udall, *Carr, O'Keeffe, Kahlo: Places of Their Own*, 259.

[8] Sherrill Grace, "From Emily Carr to Joy Coghill... and Back: Writing the Self in *Song of this Place*", April 2003 unpublished manuscript, 15.

Cynthia Zimmerman teaches a variety of English Literature and Drama Studies courses at Glendon, York University's bilingual college. She has published a number of books plus articles, chapters and public papers specializing in the work of Canadian women playwrights. She remembers being enchanted as a child by plays performed at UBC when Joy Coghill was the founding Artistic Director of Holiday Theatre, Canada's first professional children's theatre company.

— • — *Playwright's Notes and Acknowledgements* — • —

by Joy Coghill

When any Canadian actress reaches her fifty-sixth year, she develops a passionate desire to play Emily Carr. The initial impulse has a lot to do with the fascinating fact that Emily did her best work after the age of fifty-six. That is the first of many mysteries, for Carr overcame insuperable obstacles to become Canada's most famous woman artist.

When the Carr passion strikes, leading actresses usually request or commission a distinguished writer to create a play for them. I was no exception. Rather arrogantly, I went to the "*crème de la crème.*" I am grateful that P.K. Page and Alice Munro were kind but said, "No. You must do it yourself," and that John Murrell offered me the chance to try my hand at the Banff Playwright's Colony.

There, in the spring of 1984, I suffered agonies wrestling with the spirit of Emily Carr. Through the wall I could hear real playwrights like Paul Gross typing away at two hundred words a minute, while I pushed my pencil across my pad of yellow-lined paper. However, it was in Banff that Maria Campbell advised, "Listen to the voice of the Grandmother." And it was there where I told Emily that most Canadians did not go to art galleries and that to be an artist today was just as much of a struggle as it was in her time. "Silly buggers," said Millie Carr at two in the morning. And so the play took shape as the story of an actress who wanted to play Emily, while Emily refuses to let her.

I was haunted, not only by the ghost of Emily Carr, but also by the actor's playwright, Anton Chekhov. In his play, *The Seagull*, the young playwright Treplev declares that the theatre has become dull, boring, and in dire need of "new forms." When I reached for "new forms," I was led to the innovative work of Felix Mirbt and his puppet dramas, *Woyzeck* and *The Dream Play*.

The creative magus of *Song of This Place* was Robert More, who had trained with Mirbt. He took the play, and with the collaboration of artists Sherrard Grauer and Frank Rader, created a *mise en scène* of transformatory images that were intensely evocative and theatrical. He challenged and trained actors to move smoothly from mask to puppet to dance. At the same time, Bill Henderson created a score where improvised music fused seamlessly with scored music and songs. The whole was fluid and magical. Together we believed that the art of acting was not what any one actor did but what happened between them. So we peopled the "space between" the actor, Frieda, and the artist, Millie Carr, with the puppet characters and entities from Carr's life. We felt we were creating a new form of theatre that made extraordinary demands and was deeply satisfying.

Song of This Place would not have been possible without the insight and professionalism of Joan Orenstein and her definitive creation of Emily Carr. The play belongs to her and to Sarah Orenstein, Debra Thorne, Allan Zinyk, Valley Hennel King, John Thorne, and Alma Lee, all of whom contributed immeasurably to the first production.

We are all indebted to Roderick Menzies who was the first director and to Douglas Welch, who interpreted Sherrard Grauer's work, and who took us into the theatre. To our first audiences on Haida Gwaii, which gave us the courage to go on – thank you!

Neither the workshop nor the production could have taken place without the generous support of The Banff Playwright's Colony, the Canada Council for the Arts, the Vancouver Foundation, the Van Dusen Foundation, The McLean Foundation, The Leon and Thea Koerner Foundation, Canadian Air, Joyce Lewison, and Laurenda Daniels.

I am grateful to Doris Shadbolt, David Catton, Kim McCaw, John Murrell, Jane Heyman, Kate Hull, Shimon Levy, Judith Koltai, and Kate Braid for their encouragement and to Gayle Murphy for her unfailing support.

We all owe deep gratitude to Joyce Chorney. This document would not exist without the blessing of her editorial talents and her unflagging enthusiasm. Thank you also to David Cooper and May Henderson for allowing their fine photographs to illustrate this publication.

Song of This Place was first produced at the Vancouver East Cultural Centre (following a tour of the Queen Charlotte Islands), in September 1987 with the following company:

FRIEDA	Joy Coghill
MILLIE CARR	Joan Orenstein

THE COMPANY:	Manipulators and Actors
DOROTHY	Sarah Orenstein
RUTH	Debra Thorne
JON (Musician)	Bill Henderson
MICHAEL	Allan Zinyk
SIMON	Robert More

Directed by Robert More and Roderick Menzies
Music and Lyrics by Bill Henderson
Art Direction by Sherrard Grauer
Design by Douglas Welch
Puppets by Frank Rader
Costumes by Geraldine Richardson

— • — *Characters* — • —

FRIEDA, an actress
MILLIE CARR, a painter

THE COMPANY: Manipulators and Actors
    DOROTHY
    RUTH
    JON (Musician)
    MICHAEL
    SIMON

ACT ONE
Puppet characters in Frieda's play (all voiced by Frieda)
    HAROLD
    SOPHIE
    FATHER
    CHORUS OF CRITICS
    ALICE
    BIDDIE
    CHILD
    MILLIE

ACT TWO
Characters in Millie's deeper world where the manipulators serve her—

as Actors	as Puppeteers
ADOLPHUS, the cat	MILLIE'S SMALL
BILLIE, the Dog	HAROLD
WOO, the Monkey	SOPHIE
HAROLD	ALICE
SOPHIE	CHILD
YOUNG MILLIE	DOCTOR 1 & 2
	PATIENT 1 & 2
	FRIEDA'S SMALL
	MASK OF FATHER
	BIDDIE

— • — *Note* — • —

Puppet characters are identified by using SMALL CAPS.

—•— *Song of This Place* —•—

ACT ONE

> *The stage should suggest a deep forest, the sort of space where one talks aloud, is faced with oneself, and where the spirit of Emily Carr can be found. A company of young actors enters this space. They are FRIEDA's company setting up for a run of her play based on the life of Emily Carr. They bring pedestals and put what appear to be statues on them. These are placed at random and give a strange museum-like contrast to the forest. They bring a basketful of props and place it on one of the musical instruments. They also bring puppets and masks that they place or manipulate during the scene. They "warm up" as they work: voice, acrobatics, contact improv, etc. Each person is struck by the power of the place at some point. This opening scene is full of youthful vitality, a boisterous irreverence.*

DOROTHY (*as they enter*) Well I didn't pay my union dues to become a puppeteer? What about here?

RUTH Bitch, bitch, bitch. This spot alright for you Jon?

JON nods and starts to set up his music.

(*to DOROTHY*) You're damn lucky to have the job. (*looks up at the forest*)

DOROTHY What's that supposed to mean?

MICHAEL (*somersaults in*) Tara-aah! (*JON hits the percussion. He will continue to use his instruments to punctuate various moods and moments.*) O-o-oh! And here's a marvellous convenient place for our rehearsal.

DOROTHY Don't quote Shakespeare to me, you creep. God! Will you look at those trees! To think that we could be in the theatre doing a run-through.

MICHAEL	Ah-ha but we are not... we're here, doing a run-through. *(in FRIEDA's voice)* "We must find the 'missing link.'" Ruth likes it here. Don't you Ruthie? Lovely Emily Carr trees... much mysterioso.

MUSIC: JON – Mysterioso punctuation.

	I am the spirit of Emily Carr and I come to bless this play.
SIMON	*(arriving)* I am the ghost of Millie Carr and I come to blast this play.
MICHAEL	Well, I'm the ghost of Millie Carr's monkey and I am the "missing link." *(does his monkey routine)*
DOROTHY	How's Frieda today, Simon?
SIMON	Good, good. She's staying in the car until we're ready. Set up that way. *(points downstage)*
MICHAEL	Oh-oh! What's wrong with her?
JON	She's haunted.
MICHAEL	Wha-at?
RUTH	By the ghost of Emily Carr.
SIMON	Among other things. *(RUTH looks at him.)*
DOROTHY	Well, I think we'd be better off rehearsing in the theatre. *(RUTH groans.)* Well? Don't you think the play works? I mean, what's missing?
RUTH	Something.
DOROTHY	There's always *something*.
SIMON	Yeah... but look... Carr worked here, painted here. Maybe she left something behind to be understood.

MICHAEL Simon... listen... we *know* what's missing. The jokes. I mean, this Emily Carr writer-artist person, didn't she have any laughs?

SIMON She hung her chairs from the ceiling.

DOROTHY She what?

SIMON To save space. She put her chairs on pulleys and when anyone came to tea she didn't like...

MUSIC: JON – slide up guitar neck.

She pulled the chairs up to the ceiling and...

RUTH Presto!

SIMON & RUTH No tea party!

DOROTHY I like it! I like it!

They go back to work.

MICHAEL Does she really believe men are to blame for everything?

RUTH Millie Carr?

MICHAEL No, Frieda. Millie thought we were wonderful.

DOROTHY Emily Carr was a Victorian weirdo. She was wrong. You are to blame for everything.

MUSIC: JON – A musical reaction saying "Oh come on."

We-e-ll. I suppose men can't be blamed for this play. Want to know what I think?

ALL No!

DOROTHY   I think the "missing ingredient" stuff is nonsense. And we'd all be fine if we told the story from the point of view of Emily Carr's monkey. *(points to MICHAEL)*

MICHAEL   And her dog *(points to DOROTHY)* and her cat. *(points to RUTH)*

JON   *(with percussion)* Ladies and Gentlemen. Allow me to introduce the Beasts!

MICHAEL   *(as WOO, the monkey)* This is the inside story.

RUTH   *(as ADOLPHUS, the cat)* She hated people and she loved animals.

DOROTHY   *(as BILLIE, the dog)* She loved food and sunshine and dirt and *rain*.

MICHAEL   *(as Woo)* She wanted to run around naked like a monkey and when they wouldn't let her she wore coloured sacks for clothes. But underneath she was wild... as wild as I am... and that's the truth.

> *MUSIC: JON, RUTH, DOROTHY and MICHAEL sing the song.*

> *"THE LADY WAS WILD"*

> I'll tell you the truth,
> I'll tell you no lie.
> The Lady was wild,
> You wanna know why?
> It was born in the blood
> It was bred in the bone.
> She was a creature of
> Fire and of stone.

> Chorus: *The lady was wild, wild*
> *She was a creature of fire and stone*
> *Wild, wild, wild*
> *Born in the blood and*
> *Bred in the bone*

But they said it was wrong.
They said it was sin
So she kept the wildness
Under her skin.

Repeat chorus.

SIMON leaves.

RUTH   *(as an academic ADOLPHUS)* M. Emily Carr...
famous writer... famous artist. Born in colonial
Victoria, 1871... died in... er... colonial Victoria, 1945.
Canada's greatest woman painter. Artist of the West
Coast... great forests and vanishing native culture.
(yawn) Education: San Francisco, London, Paris
(stretch) Hundreds of exhibitions: Paris, Ottawa,
Toronto, Montreal, Vancouver, *(yawn)* Victoria.
(She rouses herself.) Publications: *Klee Wyck, House
of All Sorts*, *(yawn)* *Book of Small*...

MICHAEL   Small? Who was Small? *(points to DOROTHY)*

DOROTHY   *(shrugs)* Millie Carr's "child."

MICHAEL   Wrong. She never had a child. *(points to RUTH)*

DOROTHY   I mean...

RUTH   She means the child in Millie Carr.

MICHAEL   The child *in* Millie. Hm! Ah-ha! You mean Millie
Carr when she was a child.

RUTH   No, I think it's more than...

> *At some point during the following speech FRIEDA
> enters. She is in a wheelchair pushed by SIMON.
> FRIEDA is a passionate, intelligent self-centred
> woman, an actress first, a person second.*

MICHAEL   *(as WOO)* Millie Carr when she was Small was a
rebellious rowdy monkey of a child, adoring life
and especially animals. She changes to a sensitive,
reclusive girl with only a sheep dog for a friend. She

changes to a woman tramping around the world
trying to be an artist with no animals. She changes
to a really eccentric interesting old lady surrounded
by dogs and cats and birds, and then ta-a-rah, she
gets a monkey who is fun and what happens? She
becomes a famous writer. She becomes a famous
artist! What was the secret ingredient... the missing
link? ME! The monkey! Lady Woo, that's who!
Cause listen... that lady was WILD!

**CHORUS OF
CRITICS**

*(manipulated by RUTH and DOROTHY, 2 CRITICS
each)*
Lonely she was and lonely she'll stay
They ordered their children to keep well away.
A woman like that could cast a spell
Or grab them all and take them to hell.

MUSIC: JON sings "The Lady was Wild."

*They all join in. They dance. They become conscious
of FRIEDA and then stop. Awkward pause.*

FRIEDA   Shall we begin?

*FRIEDA takes her cane and rises. She finds the best
position in the space. SIMON brings the chair. She
sits. She takes out her Emily Carr hair net, looks at it
with distaste and then puts it on. She takes out a
script and puts on some spectacles. Now she looks like
the Carr of the self-portrait and the wheelchair. The
company, relieved that there is no explosion, quickly
get rid of their outer clothes. They are in dark,
unobtrusive basics.*

Ready?

*The company put on gloves and become the
manipulators that serve FRIEDA's puppet play.
She has written this play for herself and supplies all
the voices. This play is FRIEDA's theatrical vehicle
for her old age. It is her way of facing the limitations
that begin to menace her.*

FRIEDA nods to JON. All music cues throughout are live improvisations supporting the text, unless it is a song.

MUSIC: JON – "The Fuschia Bush."

FRIEDA   *(as Carr at 70)* Life, even now, carries such exquisite pleasures...

She stops... something is wrong. She starts again.

Life, even now, carries such exquisite pleasures. Outside my window is a fuchsia bush.

She keeps an eye on the company as they create the fuchsia bush.

It is scarlet and purple. A tiny, dainty swaying bell. It is as if you could stick out your finger and stroke the joy of life.

As I lie in bed close to the open window there is a constant humming, a soft, fine whir. Hummingbirds are sipping the nectars—the life of my fuchsias— thrusting long beaks into the inexplicable core and essence of her being. But her bells hang like scarlet drops. Their secrets are still inside them, gummed up in a silence that even the tiny loving bird cannot penetrate.[1]

MUSIC: JON – "Harold's Song."

HAROLD enters. He is 40 and is physically and mentally disabled. He is on a short holiday from the asylum. He has a carved bird in his one hand.

JON   *(sings)*
Harold, Harold living inside a mystery.
Harold, Harold locked up in a mystery.
He knows – but he can't say,
He knows but he-he-he can't say.

---

[1] Freely adapted for dramatic purposes from Emily Carr's *Hundreds and Thousands*.

Bill Henderson
and
HAROLD,
manipulated by
Debra Thorne.

*Harold
Learns His
Song*

Mask by
Frank Rader.
Photo by
May Henderson.

This first example of FRIEDA's ability to "give voice"
to her puppets is crucial. The sensitivity between the
actress and the manipulator of HAROLD must be such
that the puppet takes focus and appears to speak.
HAROLD becomes a living entity and the audience
accepts the puppet world.

HAROLD   *(moves to get his voice and speak)* I am writing an
auto... auto...

FRIEDA   Biography.

HAROLD   Biography. It is mostly about my best... my famous
friend Emily Carr. But when I know it here *(He
touches his centre.)* I can't find it here. *(He touches his
head.)* When I think of her it fills me inside like...
sometimes like wings beating, sometimes quiet like
a bird waiting. I want to free it and I want to hold
it. But I can't find the – the – right – words....
When Millie dies *(sighs)* I will have one friend left,
Sophie. She carved this bird for me. She says the
bird is in the wood. You just carve away enough to
set it free. That is what I must do for Millie. Excuse
me. I must do this thing thoroughly and set down
the absolute truth.

HAROLD leaves and SOPHIE appears.

MUSIC: JON – "Sophie's Song."

SOPHIE sways to her song. She is an aboriginal
woman, a Native basket-weaver. The Sophie of the
famous portrait, this is the woman who MILLIE
declared was more a sister to her than her own. She
was the mother of twenty babies. None lived. She
might carry a baby on her back.

Sophie knows a lot about babies,
She's had twenty or more,
Sophie knows a lot about dyin'
Everyone went through that door.
When she goes down to the graveyard
Feel the spirits rise.
You can see the children laugh
And dance in Sophie's eyes.

(Repeat entire verse with harmony voice added.)
Sophie
Sophie

SOPHIE   Sure is peaceful in my graveyard, ain't it Miss Millie? All my babies. I sure had an awful lot of them. *(laughs)* Don't know what made them die that way. Hey! Look at that bird there. See that bird on Annie's cross? Don't that look like her spirit come to look around?

> *MUSIC: JON improvises a Native lullaby as* SOPHIE *leaves. Voice and drum, melody based on "Sophie's Song."*
>
> *The music that follows, "Land of Hope and Glory," drowns out the lullaby.* FATHER *moves in with his* CHORUS OF CRITICS.
>
> *MUSIC: MICHAEL and SIMON – "Land of Hope and Glory."*
>
> *The* CHORUS *forms around* FATHER.

FATHER   I left my family in the Old Country and just kept on moving until I found this settlement on the edge of the forest, a civilized place in British Columbia called Victoria, after our Queen of course. "Richard Carr has been a success," they used to say.

Sometimes I wonder. We had a good-sized family, all girls. The boys died you see. This was a misfortune in a world where sons were needed. There was one, a grey-eyed lively little girl, more like a son than a daughter. She insisted her way into my heart. Her name was Emily, after my wife, Emily Carr. Her sisters called her Millie.

> FATHER *and* CHORUS *leave. The company set three boxes for a table and two chairs,* ALICE'S *parlour.*
>
> *MUSIC: JON – Edwardian Parlour Music –* RUTH *and* DOROTHY *sing "Whispering Hope".*

ALICE, Emily Carr's sister, and BIDDIE, a gossip friend. BIDDIE sews. ALICE drinks tea.

ALICE is FRIEDA's best creation. She has her "voice," (her essence) perfectly. So perfectly that MILLIE Carr herself, already listening, is drawn into the scene.

ALICE Millie was always difficult even when we were children. Nobody knows the trial she has been to me, no one. *(BIDDIE acknowledges.)* Victoria is such a small place. Every ripple is seen, every whisper heard. I had to smooth so many people.

BIDDIE You had your own reputation to protect, your school.

ALICE Yes. Mind you, Millie was an excellent art teacher, and the children adored her.

BIDDIE *(sewing)* Oh, I know.

ALICE Later, she refused to teach save for the occasional exceptional—that was her word, "exceptional"— child. Oh that child! I cannot begin to describe what humiliation the whole thing was to me. There was no harm in it, I suppose, but I never quite got over it. *(BIDDIE hangs onto every word.)* Among my boarding students that summer was a delightful child, the daughter of intelligent educated parents. Millie would arrive for tea. She was so loud and demanding. The sack dresses were bad enough, but then, she would smoke—a dreadful thing—for the children would giggle and misbehave. And if one so much as raised an eyebrow she would tell such awful stories and... swear!

BIDDIE Oh!

ALICE Oh, I can't tell you. But enough of that. I mustn't dwell on it. *(She takes a sip of tea.)*

MILLIE is seen faintly as her child is mentioned.

ALICE, manipulated by Robert More & Sarah Orenstein
and BIDDY, manipulated by Debra Thorne & Allan Zinyk.
The Tea Party
Masks by Frank Rader. Photo by May Henderson.

The child seemed fascinated by Millie. A lovely
child. With more imagination than was good for
her. It was the animals that brought them together.
The child had a talent, a special feeling for animals.
At first, it was the painting lessons. Then she was
allowed to live with Millie during the holidays.

    MUSIC: JON – "Parade."

Soon, she and Millie were seen everywhere,
laughing, singing out loud, pushing a baby carriage
full of mud up Government Street, with the dogs
and that awful monkey...

BIDDIE   Oh!

ALICE   ...like, like a circus parade!

    The music is now loud and ALICE *has to shout.*

Gossip! Criticism! Eyebrows everywhere! And then,
oh dear, Millie got carried away and asked the
child's mother if, if she could ADOPT her!

    Music stops.

BIDDIE   No! *(taking* ALICE's *hand)* Oh, Alice!

ALICE   I was so shocked I couldn't begin to express it.
(fluttering her handkerchief) How could Millie think
that any mother would give up her child, and to her?
Of course, the answer was "no," but the child con-
tinued to correspond. She called Millie "Mom" and
Millie called her "Baboo" because she said she had
always wanted a daughter and a baboon. *(BIDDIE is
shocked.)* Oh my! Whatever made her think that she
could adopt that child!

    MILLIE is seen clearly now.

    *MUSIC: JON – "The Little Door," very still, very
white.*

The CHILD is there, lovely, a wild fawn. During the following scene ALICE loses one manipulator and BIDDIE disappears.

CHILD It was something to do with magic. The way imagination can fill every day with light. The magic of the little door that opens into the secret garden.

A wild bird appears. The CHILD talks to it and tames it.

"Mom" was that door for me. Time had no meaning. Work and play was the same thing. Waking and sleeping a delight. I remember waking in the night under the ceiling with the drawings of totems, the huge thunderbirds guarding my sleep, and seeing "Mom" standing at the open window, very still, staring at the cherry trees against the sky. One hand was stroking the feet of a bird, a seagull. The other was holding her throat. Beauty made her throat ache.

Music stops. MILLIE puppet enters during...

Everything was very still and very white. The cherry tree, the bird and her face in the moonlight.

FRIEDA and MILLIE puppet look at each other. FRIEDA can find neither the words nor the voice. Everything freezes, the bird in flight, everything. Only FRIEDA is "alive" in this vacuum.

MUSIC: Underscore – sharp breath intakes, gasps and long sighs "played" on the sampler under the following.

FRIEDA *(terrified whisper)* Oh God. I can't... can't, I can't find it. Everything... I have everything but Millie Carr herself! And they know it. They know everything. Damn intuitive young monsters.

Here I am Emily Carr... where are you? *(She takes off the Carr-type hair net she has been wearing.)* I am trapped inside you like a spirit in a tree. No way in, no way out, without your blessing.

Here in your forest your power is paramount and
I am at risk. My work is always like that for me but,
this time, I sense... some danger...

I should be in the theatre. They must think I'm
mad coming here. You've finally driven me mad
Millie Carr... my albatross.

I am too old for this journey. But I am too old not
to take it. So here I am. I feel like Harold, like your
dear damaged friend, Harold. *(whisper)* Help me...
please help me.

(Silence. FRIEDA gives up.) Oh hell... it's hopeless.

> MUSIC: *JON is there. He plays a pipe.*

> *We hear a sound, bird's wings and there is a flicker
> of light on* MILLIE *puppet. The wild bird moves.*
> MILLIE *Carr walks in and replaces* MILLIE *puppet.
> The wild bird flies to the* CHILD, *who comes to life.
> Everyone focuses on* MILLIE.

MILLIE   *(to CHILD)* I'll tell you a secret Baboo. Animals are
superior to people, patient, brave, loving. What
would life be like without them?

> *The bird moves to* MILLIE. HAROLD, ALICE *and*
> SOPHIE *appear.*

MILLIE   Remember little Baboo, seeing is not looking.
Inspiration can happen anywhere. Grasp the bird
and it flies. Enchant it and it stays.

> *Suddenly, as if an accepted reality has been disturbed,
> there is a flurry from the frozen puppet world. The
> manipulators' voices overlap as they speak for their
> creatures.*

PUPPETS   What happened in London?
Why lie about your age?
How did Sophie die?
What telling?
Why "Brutal?"

> *And finally from* ALICE *and with* RUTH's *voice...*

ALICE   Why adopt that child?

MILLIE   She was my family. Much more than my own were.
                 We belonged together much more completely than
                 either of us belonged to anyone else.

FRIEDA   I see.

> *Silence.*

MILLIE   *(breaking the silence)* See? SEE? That word again.

> *The musician and puppets are gone. The* CHILD
> *remains.*

Why does everyone use that word? So painful for
me, so easy for you and everyone else. No! You don't
see! The truth is that I was dead, or as good as. My
life had become an agony to me because I could *not
see*. The light had gone. It had been gone for some
time. By the time that child came into my life, I had
faced the fact that I would never be great, a great
artist.

Under the roof in the attic room, I gazed at the
Totems I had painted; at the Great Eagle who
created Sophie's people and I wondered why people
thought them ugly. I belonged with them. They
were my home.

Thank God for the creatures out in the moonlit
garden. The cherry tree was in full bloom. It made
my throat ache with its beauty. But I could not
paint it. I would never be able to paint it like that
wretched, ugly, little man, Vincent Van Gogh could.
I looked at the tree loaded with blossoms like
hundreds of birds and I knew I had failed. Fat and
fifty and second-rate! So this child would have to do
it. She would have to go "beyond the trees" for both
of us.

> *The* CHILD *disappears.* MILLIE *drops the past...*
> *looks at* FRIEDA.

She didn't of course. She got married and had children.

FRIEDA   What difference does that make?

MILLIE   I don't know but it does.

There is a pause and FRIEDA reaches into the pocket of her jacket and brings out an art catalogue.

FRIEDA   Do you remember the day that the Governor General's wife came to call?

MILLIE   Lady Tweedtail – um – Tweedsmuir. *(smile)* Yes, little Beckley Street got quite a shock. I remember the eyes at the window. I remember hoping the old boy across the street would keep his clothes on. Her Vice Highness was a nice lady... gracious. She bought this little woodsy thing. She paid $150 for it.

FRIEDA   Is this it?

MILLIE   *(peering at the catalogue that FRIEDA has shown her)* Yes... hmm... better than I remember it. Where did you get this?

FRIEDA   I found it at a flea market in Toronto. It's a catalogue for an auction. In 1979 the "little woodsy thing" sold for $38,000.

MILLIE   Thirty-eight thous... well things must be looking up for the artist nowadays, eh?

FRIEDA   Only for the dead ones. They make it just as difficult for the ones that are alive.

MILLIE   They would, silly buggers. Silly, puffed up people saying what should be. Not one of them understanding the soul stuff. Damn Canadians, manicuring their lawns, clipping their spirits... pushing back the wild wood.

FRIEDA   *(together with MILLIE)* Pushing back the wild wood.

MILLIE	Thank God for the monkey, the dog, and the cat. At least they're constant. *(She looks at the catalogue.)* Thirty-eight thousand dollars, eh? Hm-m-m. It is better than I remembered it. Maybe it's because I'm dead...
	(stares at FRIEDA) So you think you can succeed where others failed?
FRIEDA	Yes. All I need is your "voice," what you would call your "essence." *(before MILLIE can explode again)* What I mean is there's something... something missing. Something right in the centre I have not understood. And yet we share so much.
MILLIE	We do?
FRIEDA	Yes. Born and bred in the west. Forced to study abroad. Pioneers in art. Women in a man's world. And now I'm fifty-seven... no, my God, fifty-nine. It goes faster all the time.
MILLIE	What's age got to do with it?
FRIEDA	That's when you did your best work. That's when you soared.
MILLIE	In whose opinion?
FRIEDA	History.
MILLIE	Ah.... So, what makes you think that you can become me, even if I could give you my "voice?"
FRIEDA	I'm an actress.
MILLIE	Oh, dear.
FRIEDA	I am a professional.
MILLIE	Ah!
FRIEDA	I am an artist.

MILLIE   I think not.

FRIEDA   I beg your pardon?

MILLIE   Have you ever lived in the woods alone?

FRIEDA   Yes... no, not completely alone.

MILLIE   Have you ever seen any of the totems up north?

FRIEDA   Yes I have.

MILLIE   You like animals?

FRIEDA   *(slight hesitation)* Yes.

MILLIE   Do you have any?

FRIEDA   A dog. It belongs to my daughter.

MILLIE   You don't have one yourself?

FRIEDA   No.

MILLIE   That's not the same thing. One dog is not the same as a whole life full of creatures.

FRIEDA   I don't see what that's got to do...

MILLIE   So you have a dog and a daughter. Then you must have a husband.

FRIEDA   No.

MILLIE   No?

FRIEDA   No, I've had two. But no, I don't have one now.

MILLIE   Two? Two husbands? Well it's none of my business, but ...

FRIEDA   That's right. It's none of your business.

Joy Coghill as
FRIEDA and
Joan Orenstein
as MILLIE.

The Meeting

Photo by
May Henderson.

MILLIE	Well, I like that! Your life is a private affair, but you want to try mine on in public. You want to try it on and parade around in it. You want to live off my soul by trying on my life.
FRIEDA	To be honest... in the beginning all I wanted was a part to play. And your name was good box-office.
MILLIE	Box-office?
FRIEDA	Yes. The public would certainly pay to see the lonely misunderstood little lady, the feisty oddball who swore and smoked and flipped chairs to the ceiling. But that was long ago...
MILLIE	I was right. Second-hand... that's what your theatre is... second-hand living! I'm sorry but it's no good. There are certain things that cannot be shown... personal things that you could never understand. There are soul things that cannot be expressed. And to be an artist, my dear actress person, means discipline and work, work and discipline... detail, detail, detail! Not airy-fairy second-hand living.
FRIEDA	Thank you very much for the lecture Miss Carr. I presume you realize how insulting it is to suggest that I know nothing of discipline and detail.
MILLIE	It's more than that. There are certain people that can never, never know what it was like to be Emily Carr.
FRIEDA	Fine, fine. I spend a great piece of my life writing a play about you and you think you can just turn up and stop it. That's what you want to do isn't it? Stop me the way you stopped all the others. Well, you aren't going to stop this play... not now.
MILLIE	It's my life.
FRIEDA	Oh, no. This is *based* on your life, that's all. Your life is just the inspiration for this one. You know what that means? You just inspire. You don't start interfering and making strange noises and actually appearing.

MILLIE	If they want to know about me, let them look at my work.
FRIEDA	*(at the same time)* "Look at my work!" Why do you keep saying that? They don't, Millie Carr! There's a whole generation out there that have never heard of you let alone looked at your work. *(MILLIE waves the catalogue.)* And I'm not talking about millionaires with $38,000. I'm talking about the ordinary Canadians who go to my theatre. Oh! I'm going mad. You've finally driven me mad. You hate actors and the theatre. That's it, isn't it? You think we are all weirdos. Well, forgive me, but for the classical weirdo of Canada's west coast, you certainly surprise me. JUST GO AWAY! Go back wherever you came from. I'll just have to find the missing thing – the "voice" in myself. Go back to being famous. Famous and dead.
MILLIE	*(off again)* FAME! You call what I had, fame? You're as bad as all the rest. Sophie says, "You're famous now Miss Millie. You're my famous friend." Alice says, "Why aren't you happy dear? They say you're famous now." The vicar says, "Well, here is our famous Miss Carr!" Famous? In Victoria? Do you know what that means? It means a card from the Governor General's wife at Christmas. It means tea at the Empress Hotel with the tabby cats from that arty-farty-craft society. It means a man, a painter, telling me that women can't paint. That faculty is the exclusive property of men. Only, he says, I am the exception! Isn't that kind? I am the exception! Different, that's me. As a painter, different! As a person, different! Odd! Strange! A stranger in my family. A stranger in my town. "Millie, dear, why don't you do something with your life?" "What do you mean, Miss Carr?" "Well! Did you hear what she said? Fascinating." Pushing into my house. Into my privacy. To see the oddity with her dogs and her birds and, my God, a monkey! Famous in Victoria? I'll tell you what it means... it means unutterable, inexplicable, complete loneliness!

FRIEDA   But I understand that. That is the loneliness of trying to express the... essence. The loneliness of the artist.

MILLIE   No! Mine. MINE! You don't understand. No one understood. I never had anyone of my own. Everyone treated me as a freak. So why are you interested?

FRIEDA   Because, because you struggled and fought and won. Because there is a poem that goes...

How is it that
one star, alone,
dares. How does he dare;
for heaven's sake.
One star alone. I
would not dare. And I
am, as a matter
of fact, not alone.[2]

You were that star for me, Millie Carr. I wanted to understand you, and – and love you. And I wanted my audience to understand and love you.

Silence. MILLIE is overwhelmed by this declaration. Finally she mutters.

MILLIE   Well... that's.... sentimental rubbish.

FRIEDA   *(very small)* What?

MILLIE   *(defensively)* Sentimental rubbish.

FRIEDA   *(when she can speak)* You... you stupid old woman! How dare you say that to me. You, who lived on sentimental rubbish! I know. I've been drowning in it for years. All that stuff you wrote about music boxes and rose leaves, and tramping uphill without a single chum, lonely as a raindrop. Sentimental rubbish? You know what your problem is?

---

[2] "How Is It That One Star" Copyright © Nathan Zach 1967.
Against Parting, Northern House. Translation by Jon Silkin.

You're afraid; even now you can't.... *(stopping in flight and then rushing on)* God! I think I've discovered something new, now that I don't care, now that I don't want to go on. You pushed them away, didn't you? You pushed everyone away. Show any love for Millie Carr and watch out! She'll cut you down; she'll run away because she is *incapable of receiving love!* Now there is a subject for a play. But I'm not interested any more. That's it. Finished. Go back where you came from.

> *There is silence as MILLIE regards FRIEDA. Suddenly MILLIE chuckles.*

MILLIE   Well! So... you've got some spunk after all. And you may be right about love. But I don't think that's the subject for your play. Well, perhaps it's part of it. Actually, I don't think many people can... er, "receive love." What about you, Miss Frieda? *(She makes a decision.)* Well, let's get on with it. Be Alice. Go on Miss Actress Person, let's run a test. Alice and love. Let's see if you understand Alice, my dear good and very loving sister. If you can understand Alice, perhaps you might understand me. Go on.

> *Music: Busy sounds. Manipulators bring in a telephone. FRIEDA glares. ALICE enters; she picks up the phone and waits for FRIEDA to give her a voice. Silence – finally FRIEDA speaks for ALICE.*

ALICE   *(into the phone)* My dear, she's deaf and I'm blind and we both pretend we're not. *(MILLIE looks around sharply.)* This new book of Millie's about the family... it has upset me so much I can't think. All this public exposure... it's such an embarrassment.

> *The MILLIE puppet has entered and stares at ALICE. ALICE sees MILLIE puppet.*

Oh my dear, Millie's here now. I'll call back. *(She dusts vigorously.)*

> *MILLIE welcomes this indirect way of communicating and provides the voice for the MILLIE puppet.*

MILLIE	Alice! Have you read it?
ALICE	What dear?
MILLIE	Have you read *The Book of Small*?
ALICE	Yes, dear. *(dusting)* Yes, of course.
MILLIE	Well?
ALICE	*(pause)* It's very nice dear.
MILLIE	Nice? Nice, well that's typical, I must say. Typical. *(She cries.)*
ALICE	Please, Millie. Don't upset yourself. *(pats her)* Think of all those lovely things they are saying in the newspapers.
MILLIE	Critics and society women. Moth-eaten, mangy tabby cats and tomcats spitting venom. Snouting around my house, pigging into my privacy.
ALICE	*(very sharp)* Millie, stop that. I... I'm sorry but sometimes you... quite often you talk about people as if they were animals, and animals as if they were human beings. It makes me feel quite ill.
MILLIE	Alice, I'll tell you a secret. Animals are superior to people.
ALICE	*(repulsed)* Oh.
MILLIE	Besides, I've given them up, haven't I. The only things that loved me. The dogs and the rat and the monkey. Oh God!
ALICE	Millie, please don't upset yourself. After all, you do have Adolphus and, and all those birds.
MILLIE	I know. I know, and you hate them all!
ALICE	Millie, you stop that. *(crosses to her)* You are mean and ungrateful. Maybe I don't love them, but I've given up my house to them, haven't I?

ALICE, manipulated by Robert More.
Alice Dusting
Mask by Frank Rader. Photo by May Henderson.

MILLIE	*(suddenly grasping ALICE's hand)* So what's wrong with it?
ALICE	What dear?
MILLIE	The book. *The Book of Small.*
ALICE	I don't want to talk about it. *(starts to leave)*
MILLIE	Alice, DON'T DO THAT!

MILLIE stops using the puppet test and talks directly to FRIEDA.

MILLIE	She would do that. She would close up like a cat, and walk out. Just when it came to the crunch... the feelings... the human feelings... the important things... when there might be a real...
FRIEDA	And she'd say it was all her fault, of course. That it was always her fault.
MILLIE	Oh yes! And I'd say, "Oh no! It's MINE!" Oh God, every time. And then I'd ask her to just tell me what she THOUGHT... that anything was better than "NICE."
FRIEDA	And she'd say "Oh no... you'll probably fly off the handle again."
MILLIE	Yes, yes. And then finally she'd give me her opinion of *The Book of Small*. *(pause)* Well go on, what was her opinion?

FRIEDA accepts the challenge and acts as ALICE and MILLIE becomes her younger self with relish.

FRIEDA	*(as ALICE)* Well Millie, it's just not true. It's all a fairy tale, with you the fairy princess, and all the rest of us, ogres and dragons.
MILLIE	Rubbish, that's rubbish. Small was rebellious and naughty and dirty and separate and different. She was made to feel that way. Some princess!

FRIEDA (*as ALICE*) But you made all those things seem good – good qualities! And all the rest of us were wrong. And don't be ridiculous talking about "Small" when it was you, Millie. You were "Small." You held us up to ridicule. None of us were the way you said. We were an ordinary family. After all, blood is thicker...

MILLIE Than water? Not true! That's not true Alice. I have known people closer to me than my family. Real sisters they were.

> *The puppets and their manipulators gather, fascinated. They begin to have a life of their own. They take on the voices of their manipulators.*

FRIEDA (*as ALICE*) Millie, if you bring up that poor Native person again!

MILLIE She has a name. Sophie.

> *SOPHIE appears. She has the voice of her manipulator.*

SOPHIE You gotta go deeper into the forest, Miss Millie. That way you get to know the totems of my people better. You got to go real deep till you find your own totem. Then you go deeper still until you see your ancestors coming towards you. If you go deep enough, your ancestors and mine will be one family.

FRIEDA (*as ALICE*) And Father. Father was never so cold and stern and uncaring as you make him. I know something happened that we never understood, but he loved all of us, and you most of all. You were his favourite, next to mother. He died of a broken heart. That's what I think.

MILLIE He blamed us for mother's death, you know.

> *FATHER appears. His voice is that of his manipulator.*

FATHER It was a judgment on my selfishness. I wanted sons. But the boys died and the girls lived. You must be my Beauty now.

He goes, SOPHIE *and the other puppets stay.*

FRIEDA	(*as* ALICE) I don't believe you, Millie. You're making it up.
MILLIE	No, I'm not. He said that. But if I have wronged Father in any way, I've more than made up for it now.
FRIEDA	(*as* ALICE) And how have you done that?
MILLIE	By writing about him in the book... the book, Alice, *The Book of Small*. I put love in it, Alice.
FRIEDA	(*as* ALICE) Well, Millie, if that is love, the Carr family could do without it.
MILLIE	Do without me, you mean.
FRIEDA	(*as* ALICE) Millie, please. You have put us on show. Everyone is talking. Now it's all those art people.
MILLIE	I thought you'd be pleased. Why aren't you pleased?
FRIEDA	(*as* ALICE) All those Easterners and that Mr. Harris. I sometimes wish...
MILLIE	What? What were you going to say?
FRIEDA	(*as* ALICE) I was going to say that sometimes I wish you had never gone east.
MILLIE	Never gone? Never known that there were others like myself? Never known any real artists, Canadian artists? I would have died, turned to stone. Meeting those men was birth for me. When Lawren Harris said, "You're one of us," that was birth, the rebirth of my soul.
FRIEDA	(*as* ALICE) Millie Carr! Only God can rebirth the soul. I think you lost it in what you call your "work," in art and artists. This Lawren Harris... let me finish please... he is a clever man, an educated man, and they say he is a good painter. But Millie,

sometimes I think you worshipped him, and that is wrong. Lawren Harris is not a saint.

MILLIE   *(suddenly deflated)* I know. You go along to your meeting Alice.

> *The "scene" has ended. Pause.*

(as herself) You "do" Alice rather well. *(FRIEDA and MILLIE look at each other.)* Sometimes, often, I didn't want to go on. My heart hurt and I wanted to stop. Just stop.

FRIEDA   And then what...

> *The puppets—SOPHIE, HAROLD, ALICE, and the CHILD—gather to listen.*

MILLIE   You need to receive the right message from a soul that understands. I tried to put the message in my trees.

FRIEDA   That is why I'm here.

MILLIE   Good.

> *SOPHIE goes to FRIEDA. A manipulator provides her voice.*

SOPHIE   Know what? When you're after... like you say... that "song," you gotta listen to the voice of the Grandmother. What my mother calls D'Sonoqua. What do you hear?

> *SOPHIE touches FRIEDA's hand.*

FRIEDA   There are some women born to be Singers
To them is entrusted the mystery
of the Wild Wisdom
Like wild birds they sing the songs of the earth
and the sky

The Journey of a Singer is hazardous and lonely
Her silences are deeper and more despairing
than those of her sisters

But when the songs return to her
clarified by silence and despair
They pour through the darkness of the forest
The Child and the Goddess are reborn
in every woman that hears her songs.
And when the vision blurs on the face of death
even the trees dance.

> *The puppets react and disappear. Silence. The*
> *musician appears behind FRIEDA and MILLIE.*

MILLIE What we need to do, you know, is go in deeper.
Deeper. To a place where dancing is possible.

> *She whips FRIEDA around and we see her push*
> *FRIEDA into the forest. As she passes the musician,*
> *he nods and touches her shoulder. FRIEDA doesn't see*
> *him.*
>
> *During the song, the stage changes to a deeper place.*
> *Birds fly during the song.*
>
> *MUSIC: JON sings "Wild One."*

Change your life,
                    Wild One.
Change your life,
                    Make it strong.
Change the world,
                    Wild One.
                    Sing your own Song.

Now, now that the dark has come
And the virgin green was made unclean
By the foolish one.

Now, everyone has to pay,
And the more that we resist,
The more the blindness stays

Yeah the more that we resist,
The more the blindness stays

Repeat the entire previous section an octave higher.

So, Change your life,
              Wild One.
Change your life,
              Make it strong.
Change the world,
              Wild One.
              Sing your own song.

ACT TWO

*MILLIE sits at her easel. FRIEDA sits alone
watching. We are deeper in the forest where we will
"see" deeper into MILLIE's life.*

*MILLIE is humming as she goes about her old
routine of preparing to paint, looking, campstool,
looking, canvas, cigarette, looking. The humming
strengthens into a hymn, "The Spacious Firmament on
High." As she sings, her animals emerge: BILLIE, the
dog; ADOLPHUS, the cat; and WOO, the monkey.*

*The animals come close, expectant, wanting to play,
but they have been trained to be still when MILLIE
is working. She will pretend not to see them.*

MILLIE   (*singing, no accompaniment*)
The spacious firmament on high,
          With all the blue ethereal sky,
And spangled heav'ns, a shining frame,
Their great original proclaim.

Soon as the evening shades prevail
The moon takes up the wondrous tale;
And nightly to the listening earth
Repeats the story of her birth.

(*softly*) I want it so much, the "song," the song of
this place. People don't understand. But you do,
don't you. Eh, Billie? Eh, boy? Oh, yes, yes, you too,
Adolphus. You too (*bird on her shoulder*) and you,
Lady Woo. Now, now gently then. It's in the
morning, isn't it? It's between us and the morning,
(*Animals try to edge closer without moving.*) between us
and the trees, and soon – soon, between us and the
sky. A small sound like music, a whisper.

> *MUSIC: "The Song of the Space Between" –little
> rhythm sounds coming from animals.*

Each thing with it's own rhythm, each centre saying,
"I am, I am... look at me." (*Animals respond. It is what
they are thinking.*) We feel the song, don't we, because

we are the song too! We want to explode with our song. The morning is lovely, and we want to PLAY! *(The animals and MILLIE explode into play.)*

(calls) Harold!

HAROLD *(off)* Coming. *(Animals rush off to find him.)*

MILLIE *(suddenly to FRIEDA)* That what you were looking for?

FRIEDA Yes, yes. I can see it... I mean... it reveals the...

MILLIE The happy artist with her creatures? Yes, best to get it over. The tip of the iceberg...

FRIEDA I was going to say, it reveals the importance of the animals in her... your life.

MILLIE Ah-ha! Well! If animals could speak, we'd have the truth, wouldn't we? Sh-sh!

> *In the process of going "deeper" into MILLIE's life, some of the puppet characters of FRIEDA's play from Act One become full-sized actors. They are played by the manipulators.*
>
> *HAROLD enters. He is a full-sized version of his puppet self. He is happy here with MILLIE, but his mood can change quickly.*

HAROLD Good morning Millie.

MILLIE Morning Harold. Oof! I'm puffed out. How on earth did you quieten those beasts?

HAROLD Well, I gave them their dinner.

MILLIE Dinner? At breakfast?

HAROLD Yes. You see, I won't be here at dinnertime so I thought....

MILLIE Of course. How clever you are Harold.

HAROLD   *(going very close to MILLIE)* Millie, is that Sophie?

MILLIE   No, that's Frieda.

HAROLD   You never invited anyone before.

MILLIE   No.

HAROLD   *(to FRIEDA)* I've known Millie a long time, so long I cannot see her face.

FRIEDA   *(hesitant)* That's a long time.

HAROLD   Millie... do I have to... you know, go back? Do I have to go back to the asylum when Sophie comes?

MILLIE   Yes Harold. We promised.

HAROLD   But I have to work on my auto... auto...

MILLIE   Biography.

HAROLD   Biography. Yes. And I can't finish it. *(to FRIEDA)* It is mostly about my friend, M. Emily Carr. But I can't do it properly because I can't... my mind won't... she is too complicated. *(rocking, getting upset)* There is no time, no time... and I can't-get-it-right.

MILLIE   *(sharply but firm)* Harold. Listen. She can't get it right either. If you both want to get it right, start with Small.

HAROLD   No... I... no, it's Millie I can't... I can't get right.

MILLIE   Harold. Think. Who is Small? Do you remember?

HAROLD   I think so.

MILLIE   There were five girls in the Carr family and...

HAROLD   Small was the smallest girl.

MILLIE   Then there was a brother.

HAROLD	He died. *(to FRIEDA)* All the boys died.
MILLIE	Yes. Father was straight and stern and clever. Mother was round...
HAROLD	And gentle and wise.
MILLIE	But it is Small who knew the truth...
HAROLD	*(at the same time)* ...the truth about Millie.

> *MUSIC: The Music of Small.*

> *Suddenly the puppet SMALL is there and once there, it will be hard to get rid of her. HAROLD and MILLIE stare at FRIEDA as SMALL enters. Note: Only her head is used at first.*

SMALL   *(voice of her manipulator)* In the beginning was Small. Me. I am the most important part of M. Emily Carr. I love everyone and everyone should love me and when they don't, I sing very loud so people *pay attention*! And when they punish me, I don't care because best I love animals. Dogs and monkeys and cats and cows! Anyone who doesn't love animals doesn't love me! And I don't care because one day I'll do something special that no one else can do, and they'll be sorry and then everyone will love me.

MILLIE   Small. Shh-s-stt! Just tell the stories, just the stories and not all of them.

SMALL   How many? One? Two? Three?

MILLIE   No two. Just two, but fragments. Small pieces.

SMALL   *(attaches herself to her body)* Two small pieces from *The Book of Small* by Emily Carr.[3] *(She curtsies and then does it well.)*

One: On the very last bush the currants were white. The riper they grew, the clearer they got. You could

---

[3] Freely adapted for dramatic purposes from Emily Carr's *The Book of Small.*

see the tiny veins in their skin and the seeds and the juice. Each currant hung there like an almost told secret. "Oh," I used to think, "if the currants were a wee bit clearer, then perhaps you could see them living inside."

Two: All my life I loved to sing THIS LOUD! I sang to the cow and the hen. The old cow would chew and twitch to my song and slobber beautiful slobber all over my smock. Then Bigger, my big sister, would punish me for NOISE and DIRT! But one day I heard my mother and her friend singing ec-sta-tic-ly and I didn't care about Bigger. I sang to the cow louder than ever. I sang right into my mother's window. And the song exploded the morning with its SIZE! *(She looks at* MILLIE *and whispers.)* Millie, is that Alice?

MILLIE   No. Her name is Frieda. She is an actress.

SMALL   Actress! *(She stares.)* She's not an artist then, is she.

MILLIE   *(indulgent)* Now, now. Hush Small. Don't shame me before strangers.

SMALL   *(buzzing over to look at* FRIEDA*)* She's not an artist, Millie. She has no Small.

          (to HAROLD*)* Are you going to write about me, Harold, in your autobiography?

HAROLD   Yes. Because you are part of Millie. You are Millie's small self.

SMALL   I am the most important part.

HAROLD   No, I don't think...

SMALL   I AM. I was born FIRST.

MILLIE   Now Small. That's not true.

SMALL   We-e-ll. T'Other Emily was born at the same time. *(to* FRIEDA*)* In case you don't know, T'Other Emily is Millie's artist self.

MILLIE   Small, I think...

SMALL   We-e-ll SHE doesn't KNOW! Have you ever seen T'Other Emily, Harold?

HAROLD   No. She is a mystery.

SMALL   But she is REAL. Real as COWS! Millie, tell us the story of the "The Birth of T'Other Emily."

MILLIE   Ask Frieda.

SMALL   She doesn't know.

MILLIE   Small!

SMALL   We-e-ll. How could she know?

MILLIE   Let her try. *(snaps at FRIEDA)* Careful now.

SMALL   Careful.

HAROLD   Thorough.

SMALL   Yes, thorough.

MILLIE   Detail, detail.

> SMALL *climbs onto HAROLD's knee. They stare at FRIEDA.*

FRIEDA   *(hesitant)* T'Other Emily was born on the 13th day of December, 1871. She was born in the middle of a snowstorm...

SMALL   Like me.

FRIEDA   With you... you and T'Other were the beginning of Millie.

SMALL   And the sparrows.

FRIEDA   And there were birds on the window sill.

SMALL   Sparrows.

FRIEDA   All right, sparrows. And it was sunrise.

SMALL   Yes.

FRIEDA   At first there was only Small and T'Other. They were "twinned" together and when they saw something beautiful they would dance together and roll in the mud.

> *A YOUNG MILLIE enters. She may wear a neutral mask that is open and vulnerable. SMALL runs to her. They dance together.*

> *MUSIC: The Mud Dance – a joyous improvisation.*

But soon, because T'Other's spirit possessed her, young Millie began to "see" things very clearly and even hear their music.

> *YOUNG MILLIE leaves SMALL as she "sees" and hears the music.*

When she looked at the cherry tree, it hurt her throat with its beauty. She could see the world of each leaf and the world of each tree and the dance between. The music for the dance came from deep within the earth and deep within her. It was wild music. It was dangerous.

> *MUSIC: The Dance of the Wild Wisdom. Intense.*

> *YOUNG MILLIE is shaken by the music of "the leaf" and then "the tree." She dances as the wild music fills her. SMALL runs away to MILLIE. The space is full of shadows menacing YOUNG MILLIE. At the climax of the dance, a huge MASK OF FATHER enters the space and the trees fade to nothing.*

SMALL   I DON'T LIKE THIS STORY!! Stop her! Stop her! She's going to say I died. She's going to say T'Other died. She's going to say Father killed us. It's not true. Look! I'm here!

*YOUNG MILLIE and MASK OF FATHER
disappear and SOPHIE in her full-size form takes
their place. The following is underlined by a single
note sounding in the air. HAROLD covers his ears.*

HAROLD   I don't understand...

SMALL   I came back in the book; *The Book of Small* is me,
so I'm alive. T'Other never died either. We made
Millie famous, the way an actress never could be.
Tell her! Tell her what it was like.... Tell her what it
was like when we were together.

The single note stops.

MILLIE   Yes. *(quiet and strong)* When we were together, Small
and T'Other and Millie, that was when the trees
and the sea and, finally, the sky revealed the secret
of their being. That was the God in it. That is when
we were close to God.

FRIEDA rises to face them.

SOPHIE   That what you want, ain't it Miss Frieda?

FRIEDA   Yes. *(She is afraid.)*

MILLIE   *(a test)* Once upon a time I saw a bird. It was tied
to a bush by a thread around its leg. It fluttered
dreadfully. As I came near to help, it gave a sudden
great beating of its wings and flew away into the sky,
and... *(pause)*

FRIEDA   It left its leg behind on the bush. I know.

FRIEDA has passed a test.

MILLIE   *(to SOPHIE)* She is wise enough to know that she
must lose a piece of herself. But sometimes that is
not enough.

HAROLD   I lost a piece of myself. I lost a piece of my brain. It
wasn't enough, was it Millie?

MILLIE	No.

HAROLD leaves.

SMALL	You have to have a Small too. And she doesn't.
MILLIE	Hush Small. Not yet.
SMALL	Maybe her Small is dead.

SMALL leaves. MILLIE and SOPHIE stare at FRIEDA.

MILLIE	You must be very still.

FRIEDA sits in her chair again.

SOPHIE Yeah. You gotta stay still like Millie says. You stay so still that everything falls off. You let it go. And the big mouth of D'Sonoqua in you opens and starts to sing. *(whisper)* It's your own song, Miss Frieda.

MUSIC: The Death of the Puppets.

FRIEDA's puppets HAROLD, SOPHIE, ALICE and the CHILD arrive. They gather around the full-sized SOPHIE. The CHILD is in front.

MILLIE *(pointing to the CHILD)* Now where did you get hold of this idea about this child?

FRIEDA I'm sorry, I don't...

MILLIE Where did you get the idea I wanted to adopt her, that I asked her mother?

FRIEDA From you.

MILLIE From me!

FRIEDA *(She loves this CHILD.)* From the child herself. Later she wrote a book about you.

MILLIE And you believed her.

FRIEDA	Yes.
MILLIE	What made you think she told the truth?
FRIEDA	I tested the...
MILLIE	*(overriding)* It was because you wanted to believe it, wasn't it? You tested it just enough to convince yourself that what you wanted to believe was true.
FRIEDA	No, I...
MILLIE	What if I tell you it was a lie? There was a child, of course. She took lessons. But her mother, like the others, didn't like my teaching, or me. She removed her.
FRIEDA	But her book... the detail was...
MILLIE	She was very imaginative.
FRIEDA	Yes. But she had letters from you...
MILLIE	There would be some. I did keep in touch. But did you *read* them?
FRIEDA	No, but... Millie, there is a picture of you together. You... in a wheelchair. It was just before your... your death.
MILLIE	*(overriding)* None of my friends knew or met her. Surely someone has denied it.
FRIEDA	Yes, they have. But the book... is so...
MILLIE	But if I tell you the book is a lie... it's a LIE.
	The CHILD "dies." ALICE steps forward.
FRIEDA	Ah! But Alice said it happened. Alice said it was true.
MILLIE	Alice who? Alice when? Tonight? Today? Now? That wasn't Alice. It was certainly like her. It was convincing, but that wasn't Alice.

ALICE "dies and is gone." HAROLD *and* SOPHIE *step forward.*

It wasn't Harold or Sophie either. It was you. You made it up. It's you who think all that is true. But I say it is all a lie!

HAROLD *and* SOPHIE *"die" and are gone. The full-size* SOPHIE *gathers up the* CHILD *and we hear a lullaby chant as she exits.*

MUSIC: Lullaby.

FRIEDA   No Millie, please. What are you doing?

MILLIE   What am I doing? I am convincing you. Am I convincing you? Was it good acting? Is that acting?

FRIEDA   You mean it wasn't true?

MILLIE   Ah! Well, I don't know. Is acting true? How true? What kind of true? *(suddenly aggressive)* Who are you? What do you want?

FRIEDA   I want to play Millie Carr. But you have destroyed my belief in my work. You have left me with nothing.

MILLIE   *(holds out her hand and smiles)* Give me your hand. *(FRIEDA is unsure. She extends her right hand.)* No, no. Your right hand.

FRIEDA   But that is my...

MILLIE   No, no. Please listen. That is your left. Give me your *right*!

FRIEDA   *(confused)* That is my...

MILLIE   No. No! Your right. Your right. YOUR RIGHT!

As FRIEDA gives up in confusion, MILLIE quickly grabs her hand.

So you want to find out what it is like to be me, do you? One day you show them your work... your paintings and they say, "That's nice. That's very interesting. But of course, it's not true. The earth doesn't look like that. Canada doesn't look like that." And you begin to feel you might be mad. And sometimes you say, "Alright, if they think I'm mad, I'll be mad and give them something to talk about." But then that only proves them right and then you can't tell one truth from the other. You get sick and the family puts you in a clinic in England.

The following clinic scenes are based on Emily Carr's life. In an English clinic where she was treated for "hysteria," she collected songbirds to import to Canada. The staff and other patients helped her. On the night before her first electric shock treatment, she chloroformed all the birds.

Two DOCTORS appear in white coats. They bring a third white coat and a clipboard for MILLIE. She looks at them. They nod. The DOCTORS' voices will be those of the manipulators. The puppets in this scene are the same puppets that belong to FATHER'S CHORUS OF CRITICS.

MILLIE   *(as DOCTOR)* All you need is a good rest. You've been under a strain. *(She consults a notepad.)* What is your name? Hm-m Millie?

FRIEDA   *(She speaks as MILLIE. Does she dare? What will it cost?)* Carr. Millie Carr.

MILLIE   *(as DOCTOR)* Yes. Well, Miss Carr, you have been under a strain. One can tell by the voice.

FRIEDA   *(She struggles to hold her own as she is forced to play MILLIE, but she speaks from her own experience.)* Please, I must get back to work. There is no time left to...

MILLIE   *(as DOCTOR)* This "work," it is very important to you?

FRIEDA   It is my life.

MILLIE	(*as DOCTOR*) I see. And what is this "work" that is so important to you?
FRIEDA	I am an a-a-artist.
MILLIE	(*as DOCTOR*) Well, an artist! (*The* DOCTORS *exchange looks.*) And what exactly do you do?
FRIEDA	I try to... to...
MILLIE	(*as DOCTOR, prompting*) You paint, portraits perhaps.
FRIEDA	Yes, portraits... but living portraits. Portraits that breathe and reach under the surface so we can see why the wrinkles are there. Portraits that speak.
DOCTORS	(*smiling*) Portraits that speak?
FRIEDA	That's what I want but...
MILLIE	(*as DOCTOR*) You are having trouble with your subject? Perhaps there is something about this particular portrait that disturbs you, that makes it so very difficult to complete, that makes you afraid to go on.
FRIEDA	Please. Let us stop all this. My life is running out. This one has to be the best. The best I have ever...
MILLIE	(*as DOCTOR*) Now, now. We must forget the portraits and being an artist. If you are to rest, we must find another interest for you. A woman needs interests. Have you other interests, other passions? Something that you can do for the world, for your country?
FRIEDA	No. Nothing.
MILLIE	(*as DOCTOR*) Oh come. There must be something.
FRIEDA	No. No. No.
	MUSIC: Birds singing.

> *The* DOCTORS *confer in whispers, "Birds.... Birds....*
> *Song... etc. They are joined by* PATIENTS 1 & 2.

MILLIE   *(as DOCTOR)* Excellent. Yes, an excellent idea.
(to FRIEDA) We understand you love birds.

FRIEDA   Birds... yes, but...

MILLIE   *(as DOCTOR)* In particular, wild songbirds.

FRIEDA   Wild songbirds?

MILLIE   *(as DOCTOR)* Your name is Millie Carr?

FRIEDA   Y-yes.

MILLIE   *(as DOCTOR)* And you are from Canada?

FRIEDA   Y-yes.

MILLIE   *(as DOCTOR)* Then you are the one who wants to—
must—take songbirds back to Canada.

FRIEDA   But that is impossible.

DOCTORS   *(as manipulators)* Impossible?

MILLIE   *(as DOCTOR)* Now, now. Nothing is impossible. It's
an excellent idea. We will collect the baby birds and
you shall be mother to them. You shall fill Canada
with song. What a splendid hobby, much healthier
than creating er – portraits. Now you must forget
about being an artist and smile little Bird Mama.

> *MUSIC: "Just Go To Pieces." This song is a macabre*
> *lullaby that is chilling in the context of emotional*
> *illness and shock treatments. It is written to allow for*
> *the doctors' and patients' lines.*

> *MILLIE sings "Just Go To Pieces" (lyrics in italics),*
> *as* DOCTORS 1 & 2 *and* PATIENTS 1 & 2 *continue*
> *dialogue.*

DOCTOR #1, manipulated by Sarah Orenstein;
DOCTOR #2, manipulated by Robert More;
Joy Coghill (in wheelchair); Joan Orenstein (standing);
PATIENT #3, manipulated by Allan Zinyk;
PATIENT #4, manipulated by Debra Thorne.

Just Go To Pieces

Masks by Frank Rader. Photo by May Henderson.

MILLIE	*(as DOCTOR) Just go to pieces.*
DOCTOR #1	Well, it's our Artist lady.
PATIENT #1	*(urgent)* You must smile.
DOCTOR #2	Well! An artist from Canada.
DOCTOR #1	Don't worry little lady.
MILLIE	*(as DOCTOR) You don't have to worry anymore.*
DOCTOR #2	Don't worry, Bird Mama.
MILLIE	*(as DOCTOR) Just go to pieces.*
PATIENT #2	Smile.
DOCTOR #2	Smile.
DOCTOR	Smile even when they disappear.
PATIENT #1	Ahhh! *(She disappears.)*
MILLIE	*(as DOCTOR) You don't have to worry anymore.*
DOCTOR #2	Why do they disappear, you ask?
DOCTOR #1	Perfectly simple.
PATIENT #2	*(whisper)* The boys die and the girls live.
MILLIE	*(as DOCTOR) The door is open.*
DOCTOR #2	They got cured.
MILLIE	*(as DOCTOR) The time has come.*
DOCTOR #1	We do cure people.
MILLIE	*(as DOCTOR) It's no use fighting.*
DOCTOR #2	Or sometimes they die.
MILLIE	*(as DOCTOR) You're all undone.*

DOCTOR #1	People die, you know.
MILLIE	*(as DOCTOR) Close your eyes.*
DOCTOR #1	Oh yes, yes, yes.
MILLIE	*(as DOCTOR) And let it come.*
DOCTOR #2	Very common, death.
PATIENT #2	Ahhh! *(She disappears.)*
MILLIE	*(as DOCTOR) Your heart is aching, you're far from home*
DOCTOR #1	Now you know the reason why you are here?
MILLIE	*(as DOCTOR) We're here to help you. You're not alone.*
FRIEDA	I want to be an Artist. And when I doubt I can, I despair and I want to die.
MILLIE	*(as DOCTOR) So, close your eyes.*
DOCTOR #1	Ah yes. Very common, particularly in women.
MILLIE	*(as DOCTOR) Close your eyes.*
DOCTOR #2	Particularly women of a certain age.
MILLIE	*(as DOCTOR) And let it come.*
DOCTOR #1	But no one ever died of being an Artist.
DOCTOR #2	No, no. Ridiculous to die of being an Artist. *(All laugh.)*
DOCTOR #1	Yes, yes this requires drastic treatment.
DOCTOR #2	That should suit your Canadian sense of urgency, eh?
MILLIE	*(as DOCTOR) You don't have to worry anymore.*
DOCTOR #2	That should suit your artistic temperament, eh?

DOCTOR #1	Now, you just relax and...
ALL	Trust us... Bird Mama.
FRIEDA	But the birds will die!
MILLIE	*(as DOCTOR)* Come, come, Miss Carr, everything dies. And what are a few small birds compared with your health?
FRIEDA	But the birds will die.
MILLIE	*(as DOCTOR)* Now count to ten and smile. One, two, three, four, five, six, seven, eight, nine, ten.
FRIEDA	*(simultaneously with the counting)* Blackbird, wren, swallow, thrush, linnet, lark, cuckoo, sparrow, starling, nightingale.

MASK OF FATHER appears briefly and fades as the sound of a tree falling goes to silence.

DOCTOR #1	Now you are cured.
DOCTOR #2	Now you can be happy.
DOCTOR #1	Now you can be content.
DOCTOR #2	No more portraits.
DOCTOR #1	No more portraits.

The DOCTORS disappear, taking MILLIE's white coat. MILLIE (as herself) speaks to a huddled broken FRIEDA.

MILLIE	When they had finished with me, I had no desire to paint and the birds were dead... all those small birds.

SMALL returns and buzzes around FRIEDA's head.

SMALL	Millie, Millie. Tell her, tell her. She can never, never be an artist. She has no Small. You have to have a Small, don't you Millie.
MILLIE	Small. *(SMALL goes to MILLIE. They watch.)*
FRIEDA	*(whispers)* Help me, please.

MUSIC: Lyrical and strong.

SOPHIE brings in FRIEDA'S SMALL. *She is shy but strong. She wears glasses. FRIEDA speaks as if trying to remember. A life blossoms and fades as she tells this story.*

My Small was quiet and shy and no one knew what beauty cost her. Even the weight of a small rose would make her breathless. Green things in spring hurt her eyes. She swallowed each dawn and sang it wild across the sky. *(music takes ear to silence)* And all in silence. *(FRIEDA'S SMALL looks at FRIEDA.)* As she grew, birds gathered in her blood and in her breathing. So that she felt herself to be a tree protecting spirits. This went on through motherhood and marriage as if they were stages on the way to being. And then one day this tree that was herself began to fall. It fell so slowly she had time to think, "so this is what it is like to begin to die."

SOPHIE	Listen Miss Frieda. You gotta listen until you hear the voice of the ancestor in you open and start to sing.

MUSIC: "The Star Song."

It's your own song, Miss Frieda. You are your own totem.

JON	*(sings)* Oh, my child, my daughter, Let go, let go. Plunge into deep water Fearless as seabird, and songbird, and falcon. Let go, let go. And the green world will be yours.

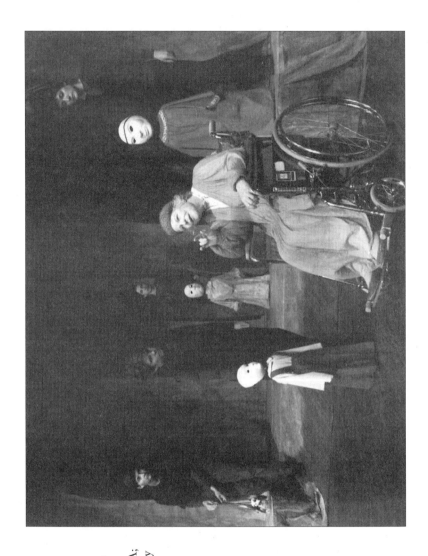

BIRD, manipulated by
Robert More;
FRIEDA'S SMALL,
manipulated by
Debra Thorne;
ALICE, manipulated by
Allan Zinyk;
Joy Coghill as FRIEDA;
SOPHIE, manipulated by
Sarah Orenstein.

*Frieda and
Her Small*

Masks by Frank Rader.
Photo by May Henderson.

Oh, my child, my daughter,
Let go, let go.
Plunge into deep water
Fearless as seabird, and songbird, and falcon,
Let go, let go.
And the green world will be yours,
And the green world will be yours.4

> *"The Star Song" rebirths* FRIEDA'S SMALL. *She speaks using* FRIEDA's *voice.*

FRIEDA'S SMALL   Before my Dad got sick and died he took me to a place way out on the prairie. The lights of the towns were little strings on the edge of the flatness. We lay on our backs in the snow. The sky was so full of stars it stretched your mind. "Do you hear that?" my Dad said. And I could. There was a singing happening between those stars and the earth beneath us. "That is the only song that matters," he said. "You must say 'yes' to that song Frieda, the rest is sleep."

> SOPHIE *takes both* SMALLS *away.*

> MUSIC: *(Dangerous) takes us to a deeper space.*

> *The chorus of* VOICES *that follow are those of the manipulators, singly and together.*

VOICES   *(to FRIEDA)* Who are you?
She doesn't know who she is.
Who are you?

FRIEDA   I'm an actress.

VOICES   You dug around in Millie's life,
You pigged into Millie's privacy, didn't you?
What did you find? The truth?
The truth about father?
Why did Millie hate him?
Did Millie hate him?

---

4 "The Star Song" Lyrics by Joy Coghill, music by Bill Henderson.

FRIEDA   Yes.

> *MASK OF FATHER is there in place – huge. It will become opaque as FRIEDA overcomes the threat of* FATHER.

VOICES   And Miss Prying-into-other-people's-lives knows why, doesn't she?

FRIEDA   The boys died and the girls lived.

MILLIE   What did you say?

FRIEDA   The boys died and the girls lived. He wanted *sons*.

VOICES   Why did she never speak to him again?

FRIEDA   She hated him.

VOICES   She was his favourite.

FRIEDA   Yes.

VOICES   He loved her.

FRIEDA   I believe he hated her.

VOICES   Why would a father hate his favourite child?

MILLIE   He thought I caused her death.

VOICES   You caused your mother's death?

> *MILLIE and FRIEDA are now face to face. This is the "transfer" as MILLIE gives and FRIEDA takes over MILLIE's "life" and memory.*

MILLIE   Yes, my brother Dick and I were his last children.

FRIEDA   My brother. My beloved brother.

MILLIE   He died.

FRIEDA   The boys died.

VOICES	He blamed you for your birth?
MILLIE	No. He said it was his fault.
VOICES	How his fault?
FRIEDA	He said the "search for a son" had killed her.
MILLIE	"I am like a bull," he said.
FRIEDA	"I have taken her life child by child."
MILLIE	"She is dying," he said.
FRIEDA	"And you are all I have left."
MILLIE	"You must be my Beauty now." That's what he said.
VOICES	And what did you hear?
MILLIE	That I had caused my mother's death.
FRIEDA	He put his arms around me and he cried.
MILLIE	I hated him.
FRIEDA	Even when he died. I hated him.
MILLIE	I wanted to be like my mother.
FRIEDA	Yes. I wanted to create life.

> *MILLIE now gradually steps back leaving FRIEDA alone with the MASK OF FATHER.*

MILLIE	What did you create?
FRIEDA	Portraits.
MILLIE	You create portraits of what?
FRIEDA	Totem poles, trees...
VOICES	*(males only)* Trees?

FRIEDA	And finally the sky.
VOICES	*(males only)* Portraits... of trees! That is ridiculous. That is useless.
MASK OF FATHER	*(voice emanating from the huge mask)* That is impossible.
FRIEDA	*(sensing the power of the spirit with which she is dealing)* Impossible?
MASK OF FATHER	How can anyone create the portrait of a tree?
FRIEDA	You have to know the tree, the inside strength and knowing of it. The terror of it. The aliveness of it.
MASK OF FATHER	*(derisive)* The terror of it!
	MUSIC: Low and powerful.
FRIEDA	Yes. How it reaches for the sky. How it protects the new growth at its feet. What it dreams. What it wants. What it is.
MASK OF FATHER	My dear woman...
FRIEDA	You have to know it as a part of you and a piece of God. God in you and in the tree and the meeting of it all! That is what I want and what I try to capture. You, you can never know the torment, the torture, the endless longing and the aloneness of trying to do that... with no one... no one to share or to understand. You never understood ME!
MASK OF FATHER	Why should I understand you? What have you to do with me?
FRIEDA	*(She hesitates, then as MILLIE.)* I – I am Emily Carr.

>*Pause. The MASK OF FATHER changes, becoming more opaque.*

VOICES *(drifting):* (HAROLD) When I know it here, I can't find it here. (SOPHIE) Babies... babies. Don't know why they die that way. (CHILD) Beauty made her throat ache.

MASK OF FATHER And you still hate me?

FRIEDA *(as MILLIE)* Yes. I thought I had forgiven you but... yes.

MASK OF FATHER Forgiven? Why should you forgive me? *(FRIEDA is unable to answer.)* Well. You are as headstrong, as willful as ever. How you became my favourite...

FRIEDA *(as MILLIE)* Favourite! You destroyed my world! You destroyed my perfect world. You destroyed God for me!

MASK OF FATHER Destroyed God!

>*The FATHER mask becomes more opaque. Pause.*

VOICES *(drifting):* (CHILD) The great Eagles guarding sleep. (FATHER) The boys died. (SOPHIE) Carve away enough to set her free.

MASK OF FATHER How do you dare to accuse me of such a thing? You and the trees and God! Is this your picture making? God and what you want, woman, has nothing to do with it. I wanted SONS. Can you understand that? Your mother wanted them too. We prayed to God for them. But God sent his judgment on us... on me.

FRIEDA I know.

MASK OF FATHER What do you want?

FRIEDA	I know the sons died. The daughters lived.
MASK OF FATHER	You know nothing. Have you children?
FRIEDA	No.
MASK OF FATHER	Are you married?
FRIEDA	No.
MASK OF FATHER	Then how can you know?
FRIEDA	How can I know love without the help of marriage? How can I know birth without giving birth? I know. Every woman knows those things. I have lived and cared with such passion that I refused all your ordinary, worn-away versions of compromising with life. I refused! I said NO! I chose loneliness and...
MASK OF FATHER	STERILITY!

The MASK OF FATHER is now completely opaque.

FRIEDA	Sterility NO! Look at my work! What I loved and what I saw I put there. Look at the small trees and the soaring strong great ones. How they enclose and protect and give life to the tiny things beside them. This is family as God intended it to be. Rooted in the Earth Mother and reaching for the sky... each with its own space and the whole singing together in an ecstasy of praise!

The MASK OF FATHER is gone and FRIEDA waits for MILLIE's judgment.

MILLIE	Yes. You are a Singer. You are one of us.

SOPHIE puppet comes in and faces FRIEDA.

FRIEDA	(*as MILLIE Carr*) My Sophie!

SOPHIE (*MILLIE gives her voice*) I go to the priest, Miss Millie, and I say, "My friend, she is white and she is not Catholic." I tell him "I do not want heaven without her." He says, "Okay, we can face God together." So, when the time comes, Miss Millie, we will. Not now.

> *SOPHIE is joined by the puppets from FRIEDA's play... HAROLD, ALICE, the CHILD, and BIDDIE. The Wild Bird flies.*

MILLIE We are sisters. The vulture trusts us and the eagle. We stroke their feet. We leave our legs behind when we fly away into the upturned bowl of the sky. If we have wings we do not need legs.

> *The two elderly women and the puppets dance and sing.*
>
> *MUSIC: "The Song of This Place."*

Standin' in this swirling forest
Blue sky rushin' around you
Hear the song and feel the power
Rising up inside you
Sing out Sing out
From the green earth growin'
To the big sky rollin'
A song of this place
Sing out Sing out
From the seabirds' callin'
To the red leaves fallin'
Back to the earth
Sing a song of this place
Sing a song of this place
Sing a song of this place
Sing a song of this place
    A song of this place

> *The end.*

— • — *Afterword* — • —

by Kate Braid

Only certain eyes can see,
only certain eyes detect
the light within
like a lamp
glowing
as it grows late.

Kate Braid, from "A Young Tree"

What is it about Emily Carr—"Millie" as her family knew her—that speaks to many of us? She was a beautiful young woman, but a very plain looking older one who ungilded her own lily by wearing home-made dresses and clamping a hair net firmly to her head. She was known as more than "odd" in her home community of Victoria, British Columbia. She kept animals, scores of them, including kennels of dogs, numerous birds and cats, a rat and a monkey. Desperately poor, she collected clay for her home-made pottery from local construction sites and packed it home—practically, she thought—in that foremother of the supermarket buggy, a baby carriage. She was charming to those she liked and rude to those she didn't, which was most people. When unwanted visitors arrived in her studio, she turned the clocks forward to hurry them along, and most of us know the story of how Emily Carr hauled her chairs to the ceiling on home-rigged pulleys so that only the few who were welcome were given a seat. She further flaunted Victorian propriety by refusing to marry and insisting on life as a professional painter—which she proceeded to do—fabulously, unnoticed and mostly unappreciated, until almost the end of her life.

Why does such an eccentric misfit appeal to so many of us? Is it that she was unattractive to her own time and place, as so many of us sometimes feel? Is it that she was unappreciated? The facts as others see them don't matter at all, of course. All that matters is the "small" in each of our hearts who often feels abandoned and unloved.

Does her appeal lie in the fact that her mother left too soon, or that her father turned out to be not what she hoped? What is it about this woman that has inspired other artists to create poetry, dance, theatre, and radio about her?

In *Song of This Place*, Joy Coghill addresses this question by daring to ask Emily herself – by confronting the icon face on. Emily doesn't make it easy. This is a drama that asks the hard questions some of us ask silently, if we dare ask at all: How shall we express the creative spirit hidden within ourselves? Can we call on Emily to help us? It's all here: the terrible feeling of difference, of loneliness that our artist-self feels, as if we are crazy if we want to create. Here is the anger and the wish sometimes to just give up, to be "normal." Here also is the knowledge of how impossible that is – or when we try it, of how much it feels like death.

Craziness or death – what kind of choice is that? But Frieda—and Emily—face that choice, and in her play, because Coghill dares to ask, Emily answers. We learn of the secret of the "Wild Wisdom."

This is a tender and terrible telling of every person's choices and of how Millie—Emily Carr—helps Frieda (and perhaps the rest of us) to find a "Wild Wisdom" within.

In *Song of This Place*, Joy Coghill blesses us all with her seeing, feeling heart. She reminds us that it is never too late – Emily was fifty-six years old when she was "discovered" by the National Gallery and the Group of Seven. Frieda is fifty-nine and already crippled – perhaps by her own fear. Coghill reminds us of how important it is to have a friend like Millie—like Coghill herself—who can take us deeper, to where the song lies, to where it is hidden. Thank you Emily Carr. Thank you Joy Coghill, for helping us see.

— • —*Appendix A* — • —

Notes on the Puppets by Robert More

I first met Joy Coghill in 1978 during a production of *The Dream Play* by August Strindberg at the Centaur Theatre in Montreal. It was an extraordinary production. All the characters were portrayed by puppets, manipulated by silent actors, while all the voices were supplied by another set of speaking actors. The challenge, for both the puppet manipulators and the actors, was to connect in such a way that all their energies would be channeled through the puppets. It was difficult but exciting work. When we did connect and did trust our mutual instincts, when we got out of the way of our own selves and allowed what was "between" us to be the first reality, the results were amazing. The puppets sprang to life. When we really got it right, both for the actors and the audience, the puppets lived on their own and we merely followed them around like loyal servants.

More than anyone else, before or since, Joy Coghill has understood the magic link between actor and manipulator that results in a puppet or mask being given its full creative life. Joy first recognized that it was the space "between" that really counted. When she asked me in 1986 to join her in an exploration of this demanding and exhilarating place, I immediately said, "Yes." What Joy wanted was to capture on stage the essence of creativity itself. And to do this, she had written *Song of This Place*, which explores the inner world of the imagination right from the start, a journey that took apart and put back together again everything I had ever known—or thought I had known—about mask, puppetry, and acting. In all of my earlier work with Felix Mirbt, *Woyzeck*, *The Dream Play*, and *Happy End*, the parameters were clear. One set of actors supplied the voices, another set supplied the physical animation – two separate performing groups.

Not so with Joy's play. In working on *Song of This Place*, the old boundaries quickly disappeared, and it became clear early on that to bring her vision to life, the performers would have to do everything. They would be sometimes silent, sometimes speaking for their own puppets, at other times providing the voice for another puppet, sometimes supplying a puppet's voice while still manipulating his or her own puppet, sometimes becoming the puppet, and often wearing a mask. In *Song*, the manipulators were pushed to the limit. They had to be part actor, part manipulator, part juggler, and part magician. They had to live in a state of mind that was totally fluid, present, and unafraid. It was a glorious experience.

At one point in the play, the character of Sophie says, "You gotta stay still like Millie says. You stay so still that everything falls off." This is the essence of the manipulator's craft – stillness. Only through this stillness can the inner life of the mask be felt, and the inner life of the performer be released into action. Joy Coghill understood this. Through her understanding and incredible courage, she created a play through which the performance world called forth the purest "song" each individual had to give. It was a privilege to be part of this dangerous, compelling, and electric world of "between."

— • — *Appendix B* — • —

Notes on the Music by Bill Henderson

The instruments used in the original production included guitar, flutes (quena, pan, and a 2.5 foot long bamboo flute for low tones), miscellaneous percussion, and a sampler containing recordings of west coast birds, piano, harpsichord, vocal sighs, breaths, and some electronic sound effects. The sampler sounds were played and manipulated from a small mobile keyboard. The organic creative spirit of the piece had the musician singing, whistling and playing the floor with bare hands.

A CD of the songs can be made available as an aid for individuals interested in mounting future productions of the play. There are also some serviceable recordings of the improvisation cues available. Please contact Playwrights Canada Press for information on how to obtain either of these.

Photo by Andrée Lanthier.

Veteran actor and trail-blazer **Joy Coghill** is a consummate stage and screen performer, teacher and director. As an artistic director she was the first woman to head the Vancouver Playhouse and, as such, commissioned such legendary plays as Ryga's The *Ecstacy of Rita Joe* and *Grass and Wild Strawberries*. Later she headed the National Theatre School's English Acting Section receiving the first Gascon-Thomas Award in 1985.

Renowned for breaking new and innovative ground, in 1953 she founded the first professional theatre for children (Holiday Theatre). In 1994 she came full circle founding the first professional theatre of senior performers called Western Gold. In 1996 she played Lear in Jane Heyman's *Lear Project*, and in 1998 she created The Alzheimer's Project, including the play *Strangers Among Us*, for Western Gold Theatre.

Coghill received honourary degrees from both Simon Fraser University and the University of British Columbia. She is the recipient of four Jessie Richardson Awards, and the Herbert Whittaker Critics' Association Award. A member of the Order of Canada, she was a recipient of a Governor General's Performing Arts Award in 2002.